COURAGEOUS COWGIRLS

Women Who Rode the Trails and Ran Ranches

Written by Sue Young

Illustrated by Katie Howerton

TCU PRESS

Fort Worth, Texas

Library of Congress Cataloging-in-Publication Data

Names: Young, Sue, 1957- author
Title: Courageous cowgirls : women who rode the trails, ran ranches, and raced in rodeos / Sue Young.
Description: Fort Worth : TCU Press, [2026] | Includes bibliographical references. | Audience term: Preteens | Audience: Ages 8-12 | Audience: Grades 4-6
Identifiers: LCCN 2026027172 | ISBN 9780875659800
Subjects: LCSH: Children's poetry, American | Cowgirls--Texas | Women rodeo performers--Texas | Women ranchers | Ranch life--Texas | Texas--Social life and customs | CYAC: American poetry | Cowgirls | Texas | LCGFT: Prose poems | Biographies
Classification: LCC PS3625.O9733 C68 2026
LC record available at https://lccn.loc.gov/2026027172

Designed by Katie Howerton

TCU PRESS

TCU Box 298300
Fort Worth, Texas 76129
www.tcupress.com

For Tasia Young, who has blazed a trail for decades.
And for Rusty, my true and trusty companion.

Thanks to Bethany Hegedus, Gloria Amescua, Yolanda Szuch, Kevin Lewis, and the Nonfiction Phenoms: Katie McEnany, Laura Kiehner, and Sara Van Note, for their support, encouragement, and good counsel.

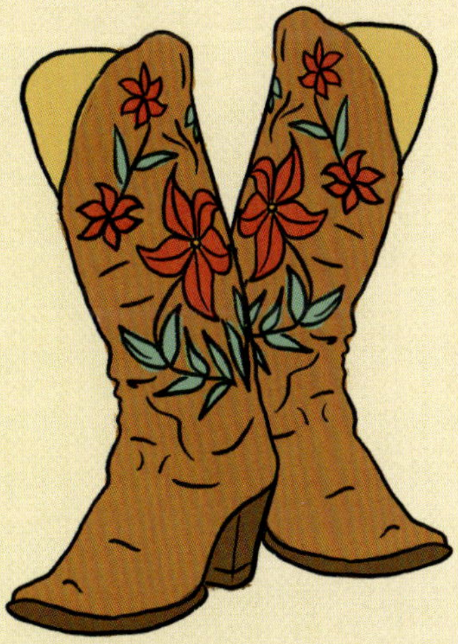

Everyone loves cowboys.
But did you know there are cowgirls too?

It's true.

Women have tended and trailed cattle.

They've mended fences and managed ranches.

They've raced and roped in rodeos.

They've shown strength and spirit.

Would you like to meet some of these gutsy gals?

Hold on to your saddle—you're in for quite a ride.

Giddyup!

IR

PATRICIA DE LA GARZA DE LÉON

Run the Ranch

1775 – 1849 | Texas

Pounding hooves, tossing mane.
Husband Martín and I ride across the great river
Into wild Tejas to claim a ranch.
I trade embroidered skirts and shirts for buckskins,
Work sunup to sundown, then finally
Our dream—a grant of land for our own town.
Martín builds the city.
I add a school and a church that will stand
For more than 200 years.
I run the ranch, ride roundup,
Oversee birthing calves, branding cattle.
I command the cowhands.

Astride or To the Side?

Women have ridden on horseback for centuries. In Europe, upper-class women adopted the custom of riding with both legs to one side, or sidesaddle, beginning in the late 1300s. When Spaniards brought horses to the New World, Native Americans quickly learned to ride. Indigenous women rode bareback and astride, with legs to either side. European women and girls in the colonies—and later the states—were expected to ride sidesaddle, but many who lived and worked on ranches rode astride.

DOÑA ESTÉFANA DE CAVAZOS Y DE CORTINA

Standing Up

1792 – 1867 | Texas

I grew up on Potrero del Espíritu Santo—Pasture of the Holy Spirit.
My ranch spans marsh to tall grasses,
Salty to sandy to red soil.
Water from the Rio Grande quenches the thirst of cotton,
Corn, beans, and sugar cane.
I raise my family in a home built from the earth.
Mules, cattle, and horses graze on my domain.
Through changing times and nations,
New Spain, Mexico, Texas, United States,
I stand strong.
When others try to steal my land,
I fight them in court—and win.

His or Hers?

In New Spain and Colonial Mexico, single and married women could own, inherit, and manage their own property. In the British North American colonies and later in the United States, husbands controlled their wives' property and money. In 1839, states began passing laws to give married women more rights. In Texas, an 1840 law gave a married woman the right to own property, but her husband managed it, along with her earnings. Texas married women finally got the legal right to control their own property and money in 1967.

for My Land

Tou

HENRIETTA "RITTIE" WILLIAMS FOSTER

gh Cowhand

Ca. 1828 - Ca. 1928 | Texas

Back bent over cotton under a blazing sun,
Hands rubbed raw from scrubbing stacks of laundry.
I am never paid a cent for my labor
Till that glorious day—Emancipation!
Free to go and work where I please,
I choose.
I ride bareback, travel
With cowpokes from town to town.
I rope, I brand, work as hard as any man.
I carry a knife for protection, but none dare attack.
They leave me be—they know this rough, tough cowhand
Will fight back.

Cowboys & Cowgirls of Color

After Europeans brought horses to the Americas, many Native Americans used them to hunt, travel, and fight their enemies. Much of cowboy skill and tradition comes from the vaqueros—horse-mounted cattle herders—of Spain and Mexico. Some enslaved African Americans worked with horses and cattle. After the Civil War, they worked on trail drives or on cattle ranches. It is estimated that at the time of the big cattle drives, about one-third of cowboys were Hispanic, Native American, or African American.

JOHANNA JULY
Horse Whisp

Ca. 1857 – Ca. 1946 | Texas

Born in Coahuila, I'm a Black Seminole.
My father shows me how to
Tend horses, goats, and cattle.
I ride bareback, black braids flying.
We move to Texas and I learn all I can
From army scouts and vaqueros.
But no one teaches me
To take a wild horse into the river,
Make it swim against the flow
Till it tires, then climb astride.
I figure that out on my own.
I don't break horses, I gentle them.

Black Seminoles

Black Seminoles are descendants of the indigenous Seminole people, free Black people, and enslaved African Americans who escaped slavery. Under the Indian removal policy in 1832, most Seminoles were forced to leave their homeland in Florida and move to Oklahoma. Black Seminoles were in danger of being kidnapped by raiders and sold into slavery. In 1849, John Horse led a group to freedom in Mexico. Johanna July's family was among them. Today, Black Seminoles live in Florida, Oklahoma, South Texas, the Islands of the Bahamas, and Coahuila, Mexico, where they are known as Mascogos.

Busi

LIZZIE JOHNSON WILLIAMS

ness Tycoon

1840 – 1924 | Texas

A schoolteacher, an author, a bookkeeper,
I decide to get into the cattle business.
I buy land, hire cowboys, register my brand.
Tell my boys to round up wild steers,
Bid on the best at cattle auctions.
Then I head up the Chisholm Trail.
I count cattle at first light.
After dusty days and campfire nights,
Sell the stock in Kansas for a high price.
Do it again once or twice. I make a fortune.
I invest in ranch land, office buildings, and city lots,
Proving that a lady can mind her own business.

The Chisholm Trail

The Chisholm Trail started near San Antonio, Texas, and ended eight hundred miles later in Abilene, Kansas. After the Civil War, a cow sold for four to six dollars in Texas. Ranchers sent thousands of cattle up the Chisholm Trail to the rail depot in Abilene, where they could ship them east and sell them for as much as forty dollars a head. By 1884, the big cattle drives were over. New railroad lines to Texas meant that ranchers no longer had to send their livestock to Kansas to reach the eastern markets.

MOLLY DYER GOODNIGHT

Mother to the

1839 – 1926 | Texas

Between North Texas canyon walls
Over waving grass and cedar trees,
Vultures circle on the breeze.
I hear the lonesome cry of baby bison left to die,
Their mothers shot by hunters
For their hides, or just for sport.
I tell cowhands, "Bring me the orphans."
I warm milk in a pan,
Feed each buffalo by hand.
The calves grow big and strong.
They thrive.
I help the buffalo survive.

Buffalo

American bison or buffalo once roamed from Alaska to the Gulf of Mexico. For thousands of years, they provided Native Americans with food, moccasins, clothing, rope, bowstrings, and more. By the 1870s, buffalo were almost extinct. Millions were shot by pioneers, settlers, and hunters. The US Army shot buffalo to force Native Americans to abandon their traditional ways of life and accept living on reservations. A few people like Molly Goodnight protected the buffalo and kept them from completely disappearing. The American bison is now the national mammal of the United States.

Stoppe

BENNIE HUGHES MISKIMON

d a Stampede

1862 - 1940 | Texas

My father gives me a heifer.
I sell fruit, save nickels and dimes to buy more calves.
I'm just fourteen when panicked cattle start running.
I jump onto my steed, ride straight for the herd.
Calm the cows, stop the stampede.
Now I'm grown and on the trail to a new ranch.
Under the darkening sky, on a swollen river bank,
I build a fire for sick cowhands.
Cattle, frightened by yip and howl, ready to run.
Screaming panther on the prowl.
Long, cold, rainy night,
I shiver and stand guard till light.

Cattle Drives

Cattle or Trail Drives could last from a few days to several weeks. It was the only way to move large numbers of livestock in the days before trucks, trailers, and widespread railroad lines. Cattle grazed along the way, moving ten to twelve miles a day. Texas ranchers rode the trails with their cattle to sell in New Orleans, Colorado, New Mexico, Arizona, and even Mexico. Today, short cattle drives are still used to move the herd to a new pasture on a large ranch.

VIOLA PERRY ANDERSON

Chuck Wagon

1864 – 1949 | Kansas

No money for learning, so I raise peanuts
To pay for reading, 'riting, 'rithmetic
Lessons in a one-room school.
I marry a cowboy.
This ranch wife rolls across the plains.
I take the reins of a chuck wagon
Carrying bedrolls, rifles, food, and water.
At day's end I make camp and start the fire,
Heap glowing coals on the Dutch oven.
Sourdough biscuits, pork and beans
Greet the cowhands.
We sip steaming coffee under a blanket of stars.

The Chuck Wagon Cook

The Chuck Wagon Cook was one of the most important and hardworking people on a trail drive. Rising before the sun to brew coffee and make breakfast, they then washed the dishes, loaded everything into the wagon, and drove ahead to set up and prepare the largest meal—dinner (now called lunch). While the cowboys rested after eating, the cook cleaned up, loaded, and drove to the evening campsite. They got supper (now called dinner) ready before the cowboys arrived.

n Cook

ALICE STILLWELL HENDERSON

Legend of the Big Bend

1866 – 1914 | Texas

Flapping skirts and bonnets
Can startle a horse, spook a cow,
And get in the way of a day's work on the ranch.
I wear men's trousers, hat, and boots
As I head across the Rio Grande
In search of our stolen cattle and my husband's rifle.
I gallop into the Federales camp, grab the gun,
Speed away. The stunned soldiers follow
But they can't catch me.
The cows? That takes longer.
My brothers and I sneak across the border,
Bring back a few hundred at a time.

Who Wore the Pants?

Women and girls wore long skirts in Europe and the United States up to the 1900s. However, those who lived and worked on ranches found long skirts impractical. Some used a long "split skirt" divided in two parts to sit astride a horse. Others, like Alice Henderson, wore men's pants on the ranch, though they donned a skirt when they went to town. By the 1930s and 1940s, women in pants became more socially acceptable.

TAD BARNES LUCAS
Trick Rider

1902 – 1990 | Nebraska & Texas

I win my first bucking bronco contest at age fourteen,
Join a Wild West show and never look back.
Crisscross the continent,
El Paso to Madison Square Garden to Mexico City.
I get my kicks with daring tricks
Vault onto the back of my horse,
Balance on my head, hang upside down,
Slide under the belly of my steed
All at a full gallop.
When I break my arm, doctors say I'll never ride again.
But I will not be denied.
Within a year I'm back in the saddle.

Wild West Shows

Young women used the skills they learned growing up and working on ranches to make money in Wild West shows. Audiences in cities across the United States and Europe lined up and paid to see performances of conflicts between soldiers, settlers, and Native Americans, and other scenes from the "Wild West." They thrilled to see sharpshooters like Annie Oakley, who could shoot a cigar from her husband's hand. They loved the daring feats of trick riders like Tad Lucas.

Savi

HALLIE CRAWFORD STILLWELL

ng the Ranch

1897 – 1997 | Texas

Perched on a sand dune
Behind my ranch house, I watch the moon rise
Over the Chisos Mountains.
Times are tough. Not enough rain,
Withered grass, starving cattle.
Some ranchers have to sell their land.
I refuse. Here I will stay.
I'll do anything to pay the bills.
I'm a hairdresser, reporter, and café cashier.
I give speeches, write books.
I'm a judge—I preside over chili cook-offs, marriages,
Speeding tickets, property disputes.
I decide.

Ranching: Not for the Faint of Heart

Drought, falling prices for beef, rising prices for cattle feed and other supplies—all these can make it very hard to earn a living on a ranch. By the 1900s, women were beginning to work outside the home. Some ranch women and men found jobs to bring in extra money and help keep the ranch going. They still do today, driving trucks, working in stores and restaurants, teaching school—whatever it takes, just like Hallie.

VERNA LEE BOOKER HIGHTOWER

Barrel Racin
Breaking Ba

My family calls me "Boots" and that suits me
Just fine. I follow the Black rodeo circuit,
Texas to Oklahoma.
Glamour Girl and I burst through the gate,
Circle the barrels,
Close enough to touch.
Hooves fly as we sprint to the finish.
I'm the first African American woman in the Houston Rodeo.
I fight for the right for Black children
To attend their neighborhood all-white schools.
I break barriers inside and outside the arena,
Remind the world that cowgirls come in all colors.

Rodeo

Rodeo has its roots in the Spanish and Mexican traditions of working with horses and cattle. The word "rodeo" means "roundup" in Spanish. The sport began at social gatherings where cowboys from different ranches challenged each other in contests of skills. Women competed in many roping and riding events in the early years. By the 1940s, most women's events were dropped from rodeos. Today, barrel racing is the only event consistently offered for women at PRCA (Professional Rodeo Cowboys Association) rodeos.

g &
rriers
1930 - 1970 | Texas

It's about time for our ride to end.

Before we say adios,
here's how *you* can cowgirl up:

Be Brave.

Be courageous. But don't be afraid to
ask for help when you need it.

Be Strong.

Stand firm when things are tough.
Care for your body and your mind.

Be Kind.

Treat yourself, other people, animals,
and the planet with respect.

Be Yourself.

Decide for yourself who you are
and who you want to be.

Happy Trails!

Author's Note

In 2017, I sang songs and told stories at the 150th Anniversary Celebration of the Chisholm Trail at the Texas State Capitol. The woman who hired me said, "You know, there were women who rode the Chisholm Trail." I did *not* know that! I knew about cowboys, of course. They're everywhere—in songs, books, and movies. But cowgirls? Real cowgirls, outside of Hollywood? I started looking and found a *lot* of stories. Women who rode the cattle trails. Women who worked on and ran ranches. Women who trained and bred horses. Women who performed in Wild West shows and competed in rodeos. I found far too many stories to include in this book. I hope these pages give you a taste of the amazing women who have worked with cattle and horses for centuries.

Women mostly worked in the home until the 1900s. They cleaned, did laundry, and cooked meals. They raised children, sewed, and mended clothes. They often grew food in kitchen gardens. They did it all with no refrigerators, washing machines, dryers, or dishwashers. No vacuum cleaners or sewing machines. Some women did this work for other households to bring in money to support their own families. On ranches, there was so much work to be done that many women ended up helping with other tasks. They took care of livestock and mended fences. They patrolled for predators and bought and sold animals. Some women took over running the ranch after the death of their husband, like Hallie Crawford Stillwell. Some grew up on a ranch and helped with the work from an early age, like Billie Miskimon and Alice Stillwell Henderson. And some just decided it looked like fun or a good business opportunity, like Lizzie Johnson Williams. Whatever their reasons, these women were as much a part of the West as the male cowboys.

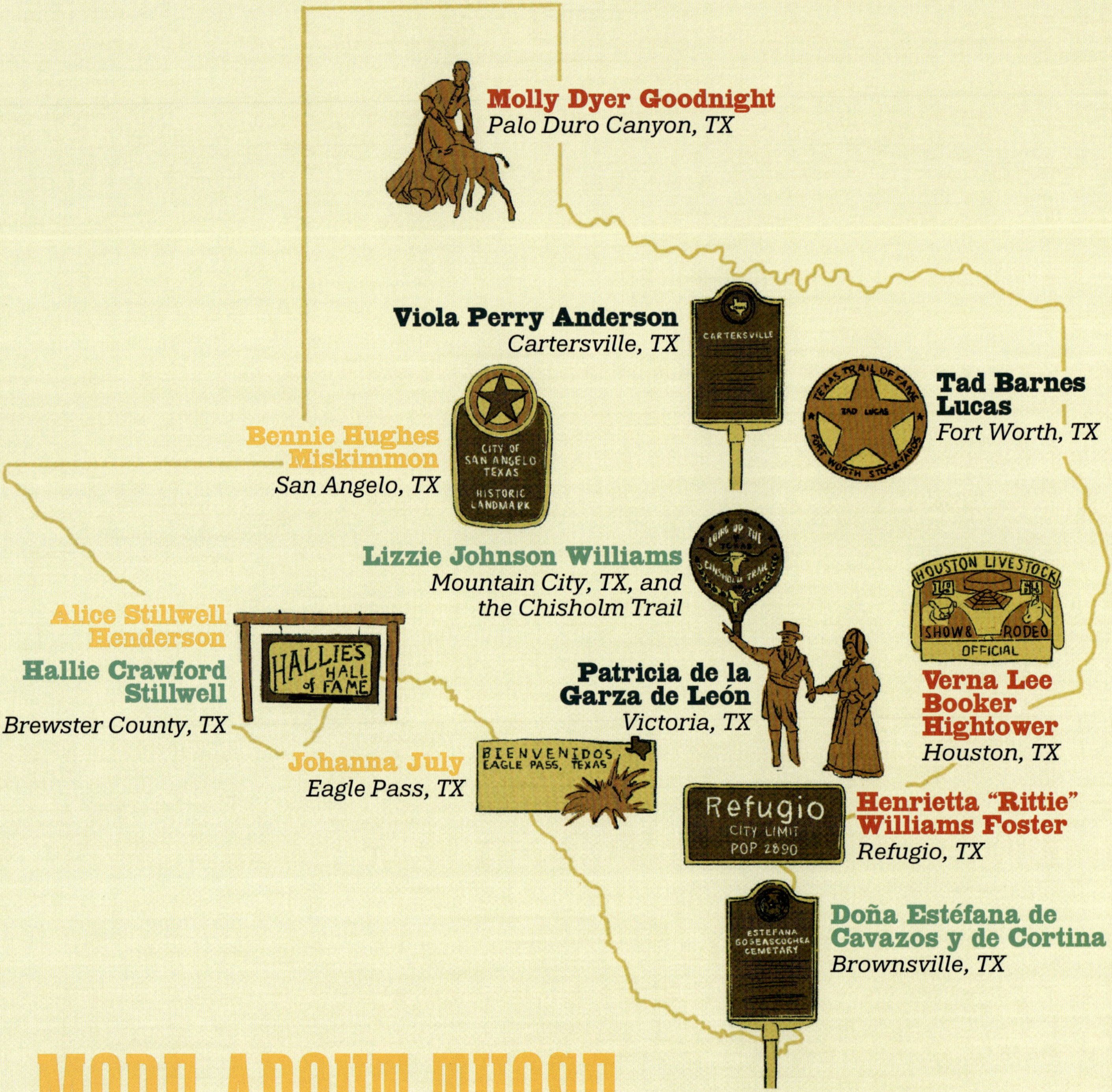

MORE ABOUT THOSE Cowgirls...

Patricia de la Garza de León (1775–1849) left her home in New Spain (now Mexico) to ranch in Tejas with her husband Martín. They received permission from the Mexican government to start their own town in 1824. After Martín died in 1833, Patricia ran the ranch and the town with the help of her adult children. Patricia supported Texas Independence. After the Texas army defeated Mexico, some Anglo settlers saw all Mexicans as the enemy. The de León home was looted. One of Patricia's sons was attacked. The family had to flee to New Orleans and then to Mexico until it was safe to return to their home. Patricia's church, now called Saint Mary's, still stands in Victoria, Texas.

Doña Estéfana de Cavazos y de Cortina (1792–1867) inherited one third of her grandfather's vast Spanish land grant. She lived through the Mexican Revolution, the Texas Revolution, and then Texas statehood. Even after she and her children became US citizens, others wanted her ranch and tried to get it any way they could. She took the challengers to court, where she won. Instead of paying huge fees to lawyers, she sold a portion of her land to them for $1. That land is now part of the city of Brownsville on the US side of the Rio Grande, across from the Mexican town of Matamoros.

Henrietta "Rittie" Williams Foster (ca. 1828–ca. 1928) was enslaved on a Texas ranch. She was forbidden to go to church or learn to read or write. After Emancipation, she chose to work with cattle. She could do all that the male cowhands did and more. Rittie's capable hands delivered babies and once stitched up the wound of a man who had been stabbed. She did not leave written accounts of her life, but many colorful stories about her have been passed down by family members.

Johanna July (ca. 1857–ca. 1946) grew up in a Black Seminole community in northern Mexico. When the July family moved to Texas in 1871, she learned tracking, how to ride sidesaddle, and more from US Army scouts and *vaqueros* (Mexican cowboys). Most people used cruelty to "break" or tame wild horses so they could be ridden. Johanna came up with her own way to train horses. She protected her stock from predators and thieves. Once, she noticed two men circling her herd. She knew they would steal her horses and might do worse to her. Johanna jumped on her horse, calling to the leader of the herd—a stallion she had gentled. She led her animals to the safety of the nearby army fort.

Elizabeth Ellen "Lizzie" Johnson Williams (1840–1924) used the money she made from teaching, writing, and bookkeeping to buy stock in a cattle company. She sold the stock when the price was almost ten times higher and used the profit to start her own ranch. Before they married, Lizzie got her husband Hezekiah to agree that she would manage her own property and money. Hezekiah got into the cattle business too, but he sometimes lost money. Lizzie always came out ahead. A newspaper writer called her "A Financial Genius." When Lizzie died in 1924, her estate was valued at a quarter of a million dollars. That's almost seven million in today's dollars.

Mary Ann "Molly" Dyer Goodnight (1839–1926) rode on horseback four hundred miles from Colorado to Palo Duro Canyon in Texas. Her husband Charles Goodnight was a partner in the new JA Ranch. Molly looked after the cowboys on the ranch and gave them medicine when they were sick. In time, she took over the business side of the ranch, keeping track of sales and accounts. She owned her own cattle under a separate brand. The bison calves that Molly saved became the Goodnight domesticated bison herd, which now belongs to the state of Texas. You can see the descendants of Molly's bison at Caprock Canyons State Park in Quitaque, Texas.

Bennie Hughes Miskimon (1862–1940) went on her first cattle drive at age fourteen. She and her sisters stopped the cattle from stampeding (running away in panic). By age seventeen, she was buying and selling cattle "like a man." After Bennie married, she and her husband trailed one thousand cattle and three hundred horses to their new ranch in another county. Her husband took the horses across the Brazos River. Bennie knew it would be easier to cross with the cattle the next day. With most of her cowhands sick, brave Bennie spent a cold rainy night patrolling the herd. She kept them from scattering amidst the howling of wolves and screaming of panthers.

Viola Perry Anderson (1864–1949) and her brother raised a crop of peanuts to pay for a year of "The Three R's—Reading, 'Riting and 'Rithmetic." When she was older, she married a cowboy and went on a cattle drive. After the chuck wagon cook quit, Viola drove the chuck wagon from Texas to their Kansas ranch. Education was important to Viola. When her husband refused to let their children attend school, she left him and took their sons to South Dakota, where she opened her own café. Viola's pleasing pies won the heart of the richest man in town. They married and had four more children.

Alice Stillwell Henderson (1866–1914) grew up on her family's cattle ranch in Mexico and later in Texas. As an adult, she herded cattle with her husband Billy on their ranch near the Mexican border in the Big Bend of Texas. There are many tales of her daring exploits. Once, Alice and Billy were raided by bandits who took food, saddles, and cows. After a midnight ride to seek help, Alice stayed at camp to rest. Billy and the other men went to recover the animals. No sooner did they leave than five more outlaws rode in. Alice held them at gunpoint all day until the men returned with the stolen cattle.

Tad Barnes Lucas (1902–1990) was born Barbara Inez Barnes in Cody, Nebraska. Her family called her "Tadpole," later shortened to "Tad." Tad rode a horse to school every day and helped her father and brothers break horses. She joined a Wild West show at age sixteen and worked the rodeo circuit most of her life. She rode relay races, bucking broncos, and bulls, but her passion was trick riding. In the 1920s and 1930s, she was one of the most famous cowgirls in the world. She rode in exhibitions and won many prizes in the United States and Europe.

Hallie Crawford Stillwell (1897–1997) arrived in Alpine, Texas, at age twelve, driving her family's covered wagon. She taught school, then married Roy Stillwell. She worked alongside him on their ranch just north of the Mexican border. After Roy's death in 1948, Hallie ran the ranch with the help of her adult children. She worked many jobs to bring in money through times of depression, dust storms, and drought. She presided as Justice of the Peace and also judged the Terlingua Chili Cook-off for many years. She opened a general store and RV park near the north entrance to Big Bend National Park. You can still visit Hallie's store today.

Verna Lee Booker Hightower (1930–1970) grew up in Spring, Texas. Ted Hightower often joked that she married him because of his horses. They bought a home in Houston near the Diamond L Ranch, an African American–owned rodeo facility. Verna Lee was the first African American to compete in the barrel racing event at the Houston Livestock Show and Rodeo in 1969 and the first African American to become a member of the Girls Rodeo Association (now Women's Professional Rodeo Association). Verna and Ted's oldest son had to ride a bus 17 miles across town to the Black high school. They hired a lawyer to fight for their son's right to attend his neighborhood all-white school. They won the case and opened the doors of all Houston public schools to children of color.

TIMELINE OF Events

1801 Patricia de la Garza and Martín de León establish their first ranch in Tejas (now Texas).

1810 Mexican War of Independence from Spain begins.

1821 Mexican War of Independence from Spain ends.

1824 Patricia and Martín receive the land grant for the town that becomes Victoria, Texas.

1830 "Trail of Tears" begins—Seminole and other Native American Nations are removed from their ancestral homelands and forced to walk to Indian Country, a United States territory, in what is now Oklahoma; lasts until 1850.

1835 Texas Revolution begins; ends in 1836.

1836 Texas Revolution ends.

1845 Texas is annexed as the twenty-eighth state of the United States.

1846 Mexican-American War begins.

1848 Mexican-American War ends with the Treaty of Guadalupe Hidalgo, which makes the Rio Grande the southern boundary of Texas.

1849 Estéfana Cortina signs the papers that help create the town of Brownsville, Texas; John Horse and other Black Seminoles flee Oklahoma to Mexico.

1861 American Civil War, also known as the War Between the States, begins.

1865 American Civil War ends. On June 19 (Juneteenth) Emancipation Proclamation is enforced in Texas; Rittie Williams receives her freedom.

1867 The first cattle drive takes place along the Chisholm Trail from Texas to Abilene, Kansas.

1870 US Army recruits Black Seminoles from Mexico to help with scouting and tracking along the Texas–Mexico border.

1871 Johanna July's family moves to Texas; Lizzie Johnson Williams buys land and cattle and registers her CY brand.

1876 Teenage Bennie Hughes goes on her first cattle drive.

1877 Molly Dyer Goodnight arrives in Palo Duro Canyon, Texas.

1880 Viola Perry Anderson serves as chuck wagon driver and cook on a 300-mile cattle drive from

[illegible] Bennie Hughes Miskimon and her husband drive one thousand cattle and three hundred horses from Jack County to Tom Green County in Texas.

1890 Alice Stillwell Henderson and husband Billy Henderson establish Maravillas Creek Ranch in Brewster County, Texas.

1900s

1917 The United States enters the Great War (also known as World War I).

1918 World War I ends.

1919 An influenza pandemic causes many deaths around the world. Hallie Crawford Stillwell loses her brother and several friends and relatives.

1928 Tad Barnes Lucas wins All Around Champion Cowgirl three years in a row at the MGM Madison Square Garden Rodeo.

1929 Stock Market Crash and collapse of many banks and financial institutions brings on the Great Depression. Many people lose their jobs.

1930 Dust Bowl begins—drought years with little or no rain mean hard times for ranchers and farmers.

1941 Japan attacks Pearl Harbor, and the United States enters World War II.

1945 World War II ends.

1948 A group of ranch women and rodeo performers start the Girls Rodeo Association. It is the first professional sports organization created by women for women.

1954 American Civil Rights Movement begins—social movement to end racial segregation and discrimination.

1958 Hallie Stillwell Henderson coauthors a book. She later travels and gives lectures about life in the Big Bend area of Texas.

1969 Verna Lee Booker Hightower is the first African American woman to compete in the barrel racing event at the Houston Livestock Show and Rodeo.

1981 The Girls Rodeo Association becomes the Women's Professional Rodeo Association.

MORE Cowgirls

Spanish Land Grant Owners

Women could inherit land that had been granted to their fathers or grandfathers under Spanish law, but some women asked the government for new titles to their property. Maria Calvillo (Floresville, TX) received a new title for her land from Spain. Maria Rita Valdez (Los Angeles, CA) received a new title for her ranch from the Mexican government. Some women bought their own land. Juana Briones de Miranda, a businesswoman and healer, bought 4400 acres for her ranch near what is now San Jose, California. Juana Pedrasa was a young Mexican widow who purchased a vast spread along the Chihuahua Trail in what is now the Big Bend area of Texas.

Trail Riders

Lizzie Johnson Williams was not the only woman to take her cattle up the Chisholm Trail. Amanda Nite Burks, Mollie Taylor Bunton, Araminta Holmsley, and Hattie Standifer Cluck all trailed cattle to Kansas. Margaret Heffernan Borland drove her cattle up the trail along with her children. Willie Matthews disguised herself as a man and joined a trail ride. She rode the Goodnight Loving Trail, which ran from Texas through Colorado and on to Wyoming.

Rodeo Queens

Mabel Strickland, Lucille Mulhall, Ruth Roach, Vera McGinnis, Florence Randolph, and Alice Greenough Orr are just a few of the cowgirls who performed in Wild West shows. They dazzled audiences and competed for prizes in rodeos. Opportunities for women started to disappear in the 1940s, so women banded together to produce their own events. They formed the Girls Rodeo Association in 1948. In 1981, it became the Women's Professional Rodeo Association (WPRA). Early women's rodeos included bronc riding. WPRA rodeos today feature barrel

racing, breakaway roping, tie-down roping, and team roping events.

Escaramuzas

Women who compete in Mexican rodeos in Mexico and the United States are called escaramuzas. Women ride sidesaddle in teams of eight. Riders and their horses perform complicated patterns at high speed. The competitions began in modern times to honor the women who rode in the War for Independence and the Mexican Revolution. The riders wear long, colorful dresses. The horses prance, turn, and gallop in choreographed routines to traditional music.

Lady Ranchers

Countless women have managed and worked ranches. Florence Johnson McIntire was a Colorado rancher who also became the state's First Lady. Eulalia Elias managed her family's vast ranch in Arizona. Kathryn and Nancy Binford—a mother and daughter in the Texas Panhandle—were expert horsewomen and hardworking ranchers. Nancy was a founder of the Girls Rodeo Association.

Some women faced cattle companies or rival ranchers who tried to scare them into selling or abandoning their land. Ann Bassett fought back against big ranchers in Colorado. When another cattle company shot her husband, rancher Susan McSween in New Mexico hired a lawyer and got justice. During the Texas Fence-Cutting Wars, Mabel Doss and Mary Ketchum Meredith stood up to the men who were destroying fences on their ranches. Mabel traveled to Austin and worked for a new law that made fence cutting a crime.

Outlaws

A few cowgirls lived on the wrong side of the law. Pearl Hart robbed a stagecoach in Arizona. After serving time in jail, she worked in a Wild West show. Annie "Cattle Annie" McDoulet and Jennie "Little Britches" Stevenson were teenage cattle rustlers. Belle Starr was a horse thief. She rode sidesaddle and wore black velvet and a hat with ostrich feathers. Rose Dunn, aka "The Rose of The Cimarron," helped a male group of notorious outlaws called the "Wild Bunch."

Bibliography

Crimm, Ana Carolina Castillo. *De León: A Tejano Family History*. University of Texas Press, 2003.

Goldthwaite, Carmen. *Texas Ranch Women: Three Centuries of Mettle and Moxie*. History Press, 2014.

Jordan, Teresa. *Cowgirls: Women of the American West*. University of Nebraska Press, 1982.

Liles, Deborah M., and Cecilia Gutierrez Venable, eds. *Texas Women and Ranching: On the Range, in the Rodeo, and in Their Communities*. Texas A&M University Press, 2019.

Massey, Sara R., ed. *Black Cowboys of Texas*. Texas A&M University Press, 2004.

Massey, Sara R., ed. *Texas Women on the Cattle Trails*. Texas A&M University Press, 2006.

Roach, Joyce Gibson. *The Cowgirls*. Cordovan Corporation, 1977.

Sands, Kathleen Mullen. *Charrería Mexicana: An Equestrian Folk Tradition*. The University of Arizona Press, 1993.

Stillwell, Hallie Crawford. *I'll Gather My Geese*. Texas A&M University Press, 1991.

Taylor, Lonn. "The Cowgirl Way." *Texas Monthly*, September 2015.

Wommack, Linda, *Ranching Women of Colorado: 17 Legendary Ladies*. Caxton Press, 2020.

Other Sources

de León, Patricia de la Garza. Vertical Files, The Woman's Collection at Texas Woman's University, Denton, TX.

National Cowgirl Museum and Hall of Fame, Fort Worth, Texas. http://www.cowgirl.net.

National Multicultural Western Heritage Museum, Fort Worth, Texas. https://nmwhm.org.

National Park Service. "The Chuckwagon." Accessed February 16, 2026. https://www.nps.gov/places/the-chuckwagon.htm.

Interviews:

Alvirita Hightower Thomas, daughter of Verna Lee Booker Hightower. Phone interview by the author, July 11, 2022.

David Busey, great nephew of Hallie Crawford Stillwell. Interview by the author, July 30, 2022.

About the Author & Illustrator

Sue Young has been on a horse a handful of times. She is a storyteller, performing songwriter, librarian, and educator. She lives in Austin, Texas, with her husband, cat, and lots of guitars.

Katie Howerton is an illustrator, letterer, and graphic designer who holds a BFA in Graphic Design and Drawing from Union University. She lives with her husband and two daughters in Jackson, Tennessee.